WHY DO SOME MOTHS MIMIC WASPS?

AND OTHER ODD INSECT ADAPTATIONS

BY KATE LIGHT

Gareth Stevens
PUBLISHING

Please visit our website, www.garethstevens.com. For a free color catalog of all our high-quality books, call toll free 1-800-542-2595 or fax 1-877-542-2596.

Cataloging-in-Publication Data

Names: Light, Kate.
Title: Why do some moths mimic wasps?: and other odd insect adaptations / Kate Light.
Description: New York : Gareth Stevens Publishing, 2019. | Series: Odd adaptations | Includes glossary and index.
Identifiers: LCCN ISBN 9781538220290 (pbk.) | ISBN 9781538220276 (library bound) | ISBN 9781538220306 (6 pack)
Subjects: LCSH: Insects–Adaptation–Juvenile literature. | Insects–Physiology–Juvenile literature. | Adaptation (Biology)–Juvenile literature.
Classification: LCC QL495.L54 2019 | DDC 595.714–dc23

First Edition

Published in 2019 by
Gareth Stevens Publishing
111 East 14th Street, Suite 349
New York, NY 10003

Copyright © 2019 Gareth Stevens Publishing

Designer: Sarah Liddell
Editor: Therese Shea

Photo credits: Cover, p. 1 Ingo Arndt/Minden Pictures/MindenPictures/Getty Images; background used throughout Captblack76/Shutterstock.com; p. 4 Mikhail Melnikov/Shutterstock.com; p. 5 Martin Shields/Science Source/ Getty Images; pp. 6, 9 Pavel Krasensky/Shutterstock.com; p. 7 photowind/Shutterstock.com; p. 8 Uspn/ Wikimedia Commons; p. 10 Garinger/Wikimedia Commons; p. 11 John Cancalosi/Photolibrary/Getty Images; p. 12 frank60/Shutterstock.com; p. 13 (flea) schankz/Shutterstock.com; p. 13 (louse) Flickr upload bot/ Wikimedia Commons; p. 14 Hintau Aliaksei/Shutterstock.com; p. 15 WOLF AVNI/Shutterstock.com; p. 16 Chekaramit/ Shutterstock.com; p. 17 Benjamin-Nocke/Shutterstock.com; p. 18 yod67/Shutterstock.com; pp. 19 (ghost mantis), 20 Herman Wong HM/Shutterstock.com; p. 19 (giant swallowtail caterpillar) Matt Jeppson/Shutterstock.com; p. 19 (hornet moth) Ruigeroeland/Wikimedia Commons; p. 19 (snake caterpillar) nujames10/Shutterstock.com; p. 19 (stick bug) EyeSeeMicrostock/Shutterstock.com; p. 19 (walking leaf) Matee Nuserm/Shutterstock.com; p. 21 lessydoang/RooM/Getty Images; p. 22 Pan Xunbin/Shutterstock.com; p. 23 (top) finchfocus/Shutterstock.com; p. 23 (bottom) Ann Kimmel/Shutterstock.com; p. 24 ajt/Shutterstock.com; p. 25 (moth) Cathy Keifer/Shutterstock.com; p. 25 (bat) Independent birds/Shutterstock.com; p. 26 Eric Isselee/Shutterstock.com; p. 27 vblinov/Shutterstock.com; p. 28 Dr Morley Read/Shutterstock.com; p. 29 Mark Moffett/Minden Pictures/Minden Pictures/Getty Images.

Printed in the United States of America

CPSIA compliance information: Batch #CS18GS: For further information contact Gareth Stevens, New York, New York at 1-800-542-2595.

CONTENTS

Words in the glossary appear in **bold** type the first time they are used in the text.

CREEPY-CRAWLY KINGDOM

Insects are small creatures, but they play a big part in life on Earth. They make up 75 percent of the animal kingdom! Scientists have named almost 1.5 million different species, or kinds, of insects. **THERE ARE MORE NAMED INSECTS THAN ALL OTHER ANIMALS ON EARTH COMBINED!**

Insects are animals with a body made up of three main parts, including six legs and one pair of antennae. Different species of insects have adapted to survive in **habitats** all over the world. These weird and wonderful adaptations mean that insects come in odd shapes, sizes, and colors.

LONGHORN BEETLE

NO BACKBONE!

All insects are invertebrates, which means they don't have a spine or a skeleton inside their body. Instead, insects have an exoskeleton, or hard outer shell, that protects their soft body. Some bugs **shed** their exoskeletons when the coverings become too small, like a snake sheds its skin.

4

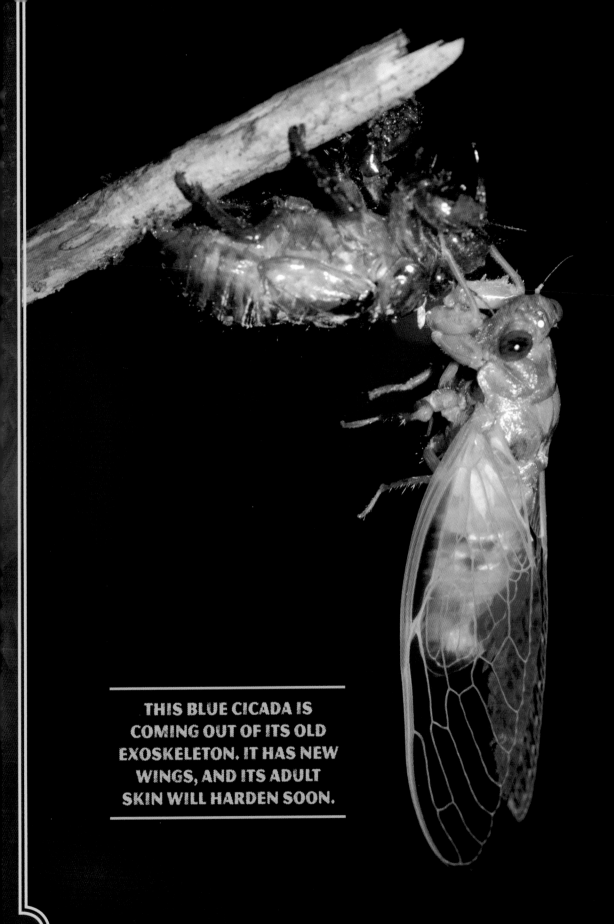

THIS BLUE CICADA IS
COMING OUT OF ITS OLD
EXOSKELETON. IT HAS NEW
WINGS, AND ITS ADULT
SKIN WILL HARDEN SOON.

HARSH HABITATS

Insects have adapted to **environments** all over the world. They can live on land or in fresh water. Some live in **tropical** temperatures, and others in frozen habitats. Insects that live in the harshest habitats are called "extremophiles." These super bugs have special adaptations that help them live in hostile places.

Proteins in the body may be one of the most powerful adaptations for extreme survival. Red flat bark beetles have adapted to produce proteins that help them live in extremely cold Arctic habitats. THE BARK BEETLE USES ITS ANTIFREEZE PROTEINS TO STOP THE LIQUIDS IN ITS BODY FROM FREEZING!

FLAT BARK BEETLE

THE TEMPERATURE IN ALASKA CAN DROP TO -76°F (-60°C). DARKLING BEETLES, LIKE THESE ONES, CAN SURVIVE IN TEMPERATURES AS COLD AS -100°F (-73°C)!

NOT DEAD YET

Alaskan darkling beetles have their own odd adaptation for living in extreme cold. Darkling beetle bodies produce a special kind of sugar that attaches to the outside of their cells. IT STOPS THE WATER IN THE CELLS FROM FREEZING SO THE INSECTS CAN LIVE THROUGH THE ALASKAN WINTER!

Heat can be just as deadly as cold. Saharan silver ants have several adaptations that aid them in surviving the extreme heat of the Sahara desert. **SILVER ANTS HAVE "HEAT SHOCK" PROTEINS THAT HELP THEIR BODIES HANDLE THE HEAT.** They can function even when their body temperatures are more than 125°F (52°C)!

Silver ants also have other adaptations to stay cool. Their long legs keep their bodies high above the burning desert sand. They always know the fastest route back to their nest, too. **THEY CAN RUN MORE THAN 2 FEET (60 CM) A SECOND!** Travelling quickly means less time in the hot sun.

WHY SO EXTREME?

Adapting to extreme environments gives insects some advantages. Silver ants can hunt in the middle of the day when it's too hot for other animals. They avoid predators and competition for food. They even eat the bodies of other insects that can't take the heat!

THE SILVER ANTS' SILVERY HAIRS REFLECT SUNLIGHT, HELPING THEM STAY COOL.

9

BON APPÉTIT!

Finding and saving food is another challenge in some extreme environments. Honey ant colonies have a special—and disgusting—adaptation that lets them store food in their desert home. Some honey ants are workers. They collect food. Others are called repletes. The worker ants feed nectar from desert flowers to the repletes. **THE REPLETES HAVE SPECIAL BELLIES THAT CAN SWELL UP TO THE SIZE OF A GRAPE. THEY BECOME LIVING FOOD CONTAINERS!**

When the colony needs food, a worker ant strokes a replete's antennae. The replete regurgitates, or throws up, the stored liquid. Dinner is served!

THE HONEY ANT REPLETES HANG FROM THE CEILINGS OF UNDERGROUND NESTS, WHERE IT'S COOLER.

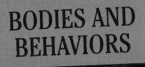

BODIES AND BEHAVIORS

The honey ant repletes' stretchy belly is an example of a structural adaptation. This is a body part that has **evolved** for a specific purpose. A worker ant feeding a replete is a behavioral adaptation. This is a special action that helps a creature or a group of creatures survive.

HORRIBLE HITCHHIKER

Some insects have adapted to super creepy environments: the bodies of other living animals! Insects that depend on another animal for food or shelter, often doing them harm, are called parasites. Their animal victims are called hosts. **FLEAS ARE COMMON PARASITES THAT LIVE ON DOGS, CATS, RATS, AND BIRDS. FLEAS USE THEIR LONG, FROGLIKE LEGS TO LEAP ONTO HOSTS!**

The blood-sucking louse's body is small and flat, so it's easy for it to attach itself to a host and settle in for its meal. Some lice have also adapted to blend in with animals' bodies. Unfortunately, they're best known for blending in with people's hair!

MOSQUITO

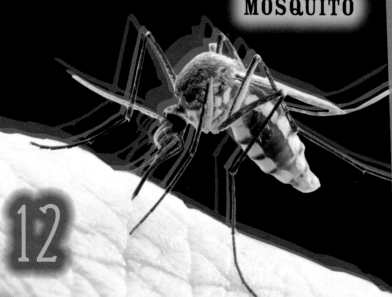

IS IT A PARASITE?

Some people don't consider mosquitoes to be parasites because they don't live on their hosts. However, female mosquitos need to suck blood from animals—including humans—before they can lay their eggs. And they can do harm to other animals, too. Some carry deadly illnesses and spread them when they suck blood.

ADULT LICE CAN ONLY
LIVE ABOUT A DAY WITHOUT
FEEDING ON BLOOD!

FLEA

13

WATERY WONDERS

If you've ever gone swimming in a lake or pond, you might have bumped into a bug or two. Some insects spend part or all their lives in water. Insects have adapted many sorts of ways to breathe, swim, and hunt in water.

THE GIANT WATER BUG HAS ADAPTED ITS OWN SCUBA GEAR! It traps air under its wings. It also breathes through a tubelike body part. It swims by paddling its big, flat back legs. To hunt, the bug grabs prey with its front legs. It uses its needlelike mouth to sting prey.

ADULT DRAGONFLY

JUST A STAGE

The dragonfly has adapted to live underwater in its larval form. This is the longest part of its life cycle. It breathes through gills and sheds its skin as it grows. Finally, it crawls onto land, sheds its skin once more, and becomes an adult.

14

AFTER THE FEMALE GIANT
WATER BUG LAYS EGGS, THE
MALE GIANT WATER BUG
CARRIES THE EGGS ON ITS
BACK, AS SHOWN HERE.

15

BLENDING IN

Surviving the challenges of a habitat is only half the battle. Insects have to avoid becoming meals for other creatures, too! Some insects defend themselves from predators by blending in with their environment. This adaptation is called camouflage.

Even within a species, there can be a wide variety of appearances. For example, peppered moths can be very dark or very light. In a species that relies on camouflage, the individuals that match their habitat the best are more likely to survive and reproduce. **AS THE ENVIRONMENT CHANGES, THE SPECIES MAY ADAPT WITH DIFFERENT COLORS OR PATTERNS TO MATCH THE SURROUNDINGS—OR DIE OUT!**

PEPPERED PROOF

During the 1700s and 1800s, pollution from factories darkened trees in parts of England. Darker peppered moths were camouflaged against the dark bark and grew in numbers. Lighter peppered moths stood out to predators, and their number fell. Years later, pollution decreased, and trees became lighter. The number of lighter moths increased!

THE GLASSWING BUTTERFLY BLENDS IN WITH ANY BACKGROUND! ITS CLEAR WINGS MAKE IT HARD TO SPOT EVEN WHILE IT'S FLYING.

17

MASTERFUL MIMICS

Many insects have adapted to mimic, or copy, other living things. Some insects mimic leaves, twigs, or flowers to blend in with their environment. Other insects mimic animals. Mimicking other animals can make insects seem tougher than they really are.

THE WASP MOTH HAS TRANSPARENT WINGS AND RED, BLACK, OR YELLOW COLORS, JUST LIKE A WASP. EVEN THOUGH THE MOTH CAN'T STING, IT LOOKS LIKE A CREATURE THAT CAN! The **disguise** is enough to protect it from predators. The hornet moth mimics hornets for the same reason. Few predators want to risk a painful sting!

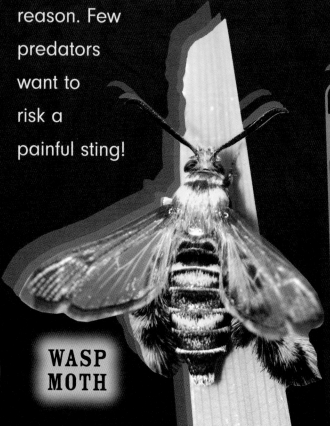

10 WASP MOTH

COPY CAT-ERPILLAR

When the snake caterpillar feels scared, the front part of its body swells up into a triangle. It looks just like the head of a snake! The "snake head" even has markings that look like eyes. Then, the caterpillar moves like a snake and scares predators away.

MAGNIFICENT MIMICS

STICK BUG
LOOKS LIKE A TWIG

WALKING LEAF
COPIES THE SHAPE AND COLOR OF LEAVES

GHOST MANTIS
LOOKS LIKE A DEAD LEAF

GIANT SWALLOWTAIL CATERPILLAR
LARVA DISGUISED AS BIRD POOP

HORNET MOTH
MIMICS A STINGING HORNET

ALL THESE INSECTS USE MIMICRY TO PROTECT THEMSELVES.

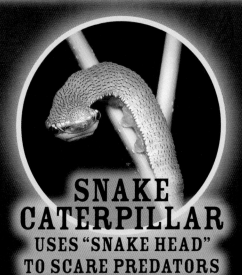

SNAKE CATERPILLAR
USES "SNAKE HEAD" TO SCARE PREDATORS

19

HIDE AND SNEAK

Camouflage and mimicry aren't only for defense. These adaptations can help predators, too! **THE ORCHID MANTIS HAS ADAPTED TO MIMIC THE COLORFUL FLOWERS IN ITS ENVIRONMENT.** This allows it to hide and hunt at the same time. It looks so much like a blossom that it doesn't even need to hide near real orchids. The orchid mantis attracts, or draws, insects looking for flowers wherever it goes. Scientists think its flowerlike coloring is even more of an attraction than its shape.

The mantis sits and waits for insects to get close. It catches its prey with its powerful front legs and digs in!

ASSASSIN'S GREED

The assassin bug kills ants and sucks out their liquids. Then, it piles their bodies on its back. It can carry up to 20 dead ants! Some scientists think the smell of the ants acts as "scent camouflage" so predators can't smell the assassin bug underneath. Other scientists think the ants make the bug look bigger so predators stay away.

STRANGE SIGHTS

Insects can look very strange, but their bizarre body parts help them sense their surroundings. Some insects have adapted their senses in special ways to their environment. WHIRLIGIG BEETLES HAVE EYES THAT ARE SPLIT IN HALF, WHICH HELPS THEM SEE WHILE THEY SWIM. THE TOP HALVES LOOK ABOVE THE WATER, AND THE BOTTOM HALVES SEE UNDERWATER!

Insect senses can be very different from human senses. Some insects, such as dragonflies, have eyes that are made up of many tiny lenses. Each lens sees a different image. All the different pictures come together in the insect's brain.

WHIRLIGIG BEETLE

DRAGONFLIES CAN HAVE 25,000 LENSES ON A SINGLE EYE!

SENSING ELECTRICITY

Bumblebees see colors that human beings can't. They can see colored patterns on flowers that are invisible to us! These patterns help bees remember different types of flowers. Bumblebees can even sense electricity. Flowers are surrounded by a weak electric field, which also makes them stand out to bees.

23

SAFE AND SOUND

Insects have adapted to use sound in odd but important ways. Moths have **sensitive** hearing. They can sense when a bat is hunting with **echolocation**, and they have other adaptations to protect themselves from these predators.

TIGER MOTHS MAY MAKE A SLOW CLICKING SOUND TO LET BATS KNOW THEY'RE POISONOUS. OVER TIME, BATS LEARN THAT SLOW-CLICKING MOTHS TASTE BAD AND STOP EATING THEM. Another moth species called *Bertholdia trigona* makes a louder, faster clicking sound. It clicks about 4,500 times per second! This confuses bats' echolocation. They can't find the noisy moths. It's a form of sound camouflage!

TIGER MOTH

LOVE BUGS

Other insects have adapted to use sound to find a mate. A male cricket chirps a special song to attract a female. It makes this noise by rubbing its wings together. How the female hears the song is even weirder: crickets have ears on their legs!

ECHOLOCATION IN ACTION

SOUNDS BOUNCE OFF PREY
AND BACK TO THE BAT. THE
RETURNED ECHOES LET THE BAT
KNOW WHERE THE PREY IS.
SOME MOTHS HAVE WAYS
TO FIGHT BACK, THOUGH!

━ BAT'S CALL

━ RETURNING SOUND WAVES

NATURE'S WARNING LABELS

Predators use their senses to decide which bugs are safe to eat. Some insects, such as the clicking tiger moths, have adapted special warnings to let predators know they're dangerous. Insects can also warn predators with bright colors, bad smells, and foul tastes.

THE BLISTER BEETLE HAS BRIGHT COLORS TO LET PREDATORS KNOW IT'S POISONOUS. IT PRODUCES A TOXIN THAT CAN CAUSE PAINFUL BUMPS ON AN ANIMAL'S SKIN. Oil beetles are related to blister beetles. They can produce oil that tastes very bad. The oil tastes so gross that predators don't want to eat the beetles!

STINK BUG

SMELL YA LATER

Sometimes, the "warning" itself is bad enough to keep predators away. The stink bug, as its name suggests, can give off a horrible smell. It may stink so bad that it makes the plants it crawls on taste bad! Predators stay far away from this smelly prey.

THERE ARE 2,500 SPECIES OF BLISTER BEETLES ALL OVER THE WORLD.

HERE'S THE STING

One of the scariest and most powerful insect adaptations is the stinger. The bullet ant's sting is extreme. It's so painful that people say it feels like getting shot! The terrible feeling can last 12 to 24 hours.

THE FEMALE TARANTULA HAWK WASP USES HER STINGER TO PARALYZE A TARANTULA. She drags the spider back to her nest and lays a single egg on it. The tarantula becomes a meal for her baby when it hatches!

The world of insects is full of bizarre behavioral and structural adaptations like the ones in this book. Insects are small, but they're immensely interesting!

BULLET ANT

NO PAIN, NO SCALE

Scientist Justin Schmidt is famous for making a scale of the most painful insect stings in the world. How did he do it? By getting stung himself—sometimes on purpose! The tarantula hawk wasp and bullet ant are tied for the nastiest sting on Schmidt's list.

TARANTULA HAWK WASPS
HAVE SPIDER-EATING BABIES,
BUT THE ADULT FEMALES
ONLY DRINK NECTAR.

GLOSSARY

disguise: a special appearance put on so that someone or something isn't recognized

echolocation: a way of locating objects by producing sounds that bounce off objects

environment: everything that surrounds a living thing

evolve: to change slowly, often into a better state

habitat: the place or type of place where a plant or animal naturally or normally lives or grows

paralyze: to make a person or animal unable to move or feel all or part of the body

protein: structural matter made by the body

scuba: stands for self-contained underwater breathing apparatus. It uses a mouthpiece joined by hoses to a container of air supplied at a certain pressure.

sensitive: able to notice very small changes in something

shed: to lose leaves, skin, or fur naturally

transparent: able to be seen through

tropical: having to do with the part of the world near the equator that's very warm

FOR MORE INFORMATION

BOOKS

DK. *Super Bug Encyclopedia*. New York, NY: DK Children, 2016.

Murawski, Darlyne, and Nancy Honovich. *Ultimate Bugopedia: The Most Complete Bug Reference Ever*. Washington, DC: National Geographic Children's Books, 2013.

Wheeler-Topin, Jodi. *Orchid Mantises and Other Extreme Insect Adaptations*. North Mankato, MN: Capstone Press, 2015.

WEBSITES

Adaptation
wiki.kidzsearch.com/wiki/Adaptation
Find out all about adaptations here.

Insects
www.dkfindout.com/us/animals-and-nature/insects/
Explore this interactive site about bugs.

10 Cool Facts About Ants!
www.natgeokids.com/nz/discover/animals/insects/ant-facts/
Learn 10 crazy facts about ants here.

Publisher's note to educators and parents: Our editors have carefully reviewed these websites to ensure that they are suitable for students. Many websites change frequently, however, and we cannot guarantee that a site's future contents will continue to meet our high standards of quality and educational value. Be advised that students should be closely supervised whenever they access the internet.

INDEX